Wilfred Owen (1893-1918): A Bibliography

Wilfred Owen (1893-1918): A Bibliography

BY WILLIAM WHITE

WITH A PREFACING NOTE BY HAROLD OWEN

THE KENT STATE UNIVERSITY PRESS

The Serif Series in Bibliography, Number 1

William White, General Editor

William White is Professor of Journalism at Wayne State University. He is the author of several bibliographies, including Henry D. Thoreau, John Donne, D. H. Lawrence, John Ciardi, Karl Shapiro, and W. D. Snodgrass. He is on the staff now compiling *The New CBEL*, is one of the eight editors of *The Collected Writings of Walt Whitman*, and is editor of *By-Line: Ernest Hemingway*, a volume of uncollected articles by the novelist.

Introduction

MORE THAN TWENTY-FIVE years ago Carl and Mark Van Doren predicted that the poems of Wilfred Owen 'may outlast Rupert Brooke's, for they are more than protest; they are poetry'; and David Daiches, in 1940, wrote: 'Perhaps the best of all the poetry produced as a result of the war was written by Wilfred Owen.' However, if Owen has been relatively neglected by critics, except for a trickle of articles, one or two each year, he is now being given more extended treatment: witness D. S. R. Welland's *Wilfred Owen: A Critical Study* and C. Day Lewis's edition of *The Collected Poems of Wilfred Owen*, both published in 1963 (Siegfried Sassoon's edition was issued in 1920, and Edmund Blunden's enlarged edition in 1931). And the same year we had the poet's brother Harold Owen publishing the first of three volumes of Owen family memoirs, *Journey from Obscurity: Wilfred Owen 1893-1918;* the second volume came out in 1964; the third in 1965.

There has been no bibliography of Wilfred Owen; although in Mr. Welland's study he lists, on pp. 151-153, the dates and places of first publication of Owen's poems, followed by an appendix entitled 'Select Bibliography', consisting of just six books containing biographical and critical information, with a strange note: 'No purpose would be served in listing here the uncollected articles, reviews, etc. that have appeared in periodical publications.' Feeling that some purpose *will* be served by such a list, I have made the compilation below. Also, for the benefit of those interested in the author of 'My subject is War, and the pity of War. The Poetry is in the pity', much of Mr. Welland's bibliographical data has been brought up to date. This checklist is not complete, but I hope I have not missed too many important articles and reviews; I have made no attempt to cite all English literary histories but have included a few representative ones. I have listed some periodicals which have reprinted Owen's poems, but no anthologies—the most popular of the poems reprinted in them have been 'Greater Love', 'Dulce et Decorum Est', 'Anthem for Doomed Youth', 'Strange Meeting', and 'Arms and the Boy.'

Of some interest, rather than bibliographical or critical importance, a few of Owen's poems have been set to music (by Benjamin Britten), some of his verses have been translated into French, and W. B. Yeats has been often criticized for leaving him out of his edition of *The Oxford Book of Modern Verse*.

WILLIAM WHITE

Franklin Village, Michigan
December 1966

Prefacing Note

I<small>T HAS GIVEN</small> me great pleasure to receive from Professor White a request to write an introduction to his *Wilfred Owen (1893-1918): A Bibliography*.

Owing to extreme pressure of work in order to complete a definitive volume of my brother Wilfred's *Collected Letters* which (with my co-editor John Bell of the Oxford University Press, London) is now in the last stages of completion so that it may be published in 1967, I feel I have not sufficient time to concentrate upon the writing of a thought-out introduction which this bibliography deserves.

I would, however, very much like to write this *Prefacing Note* of gratitude for Professor White's excellent work. He himself readily admits that this bibliography is incomplete. Indeed to compile a definitive list which would have to cover the period of forty-six years since Wilfred Owen was first published would be a major and exacting task and would entail years of research and arduous concentration.

Few books have been written about my brother (many hundreds of permissions to reproduce poems in the press and quarterlies have been given); for some reason his own published poems have precluded this from happening. The four edited editions have had vast sales; a recent edition (February 1966) in *The*

Queen's Classics, Chatto & Windus, London, which was published especially for students and schools, has already had to be reissued owing to demand; and my brother's poems have on uncountable occasions been used for broadcasting all over the world and are now being used for school instruction by television.

I would like to put on record that Professor White's bibliographical work will be of lasting value to students, undergraduates, graduates, and the reading public.

Finally I would like to send my good wishes to Kent State University and their library quarterly *The Serif* and to express the honour I feel has been accorded to my brother by starting this series with a Wilfred Owen bibliography.

I am confident that under the skilful editorship of Professor White a very high quality of bibliography will be maintained in the pamphlets to follow.

That any proceeds arising from these works will go to the benefit of scholars and teachers in American and English literature is an especially pleasing thought to me.

HAROLD OWEN, F. R. S. L.

Rodgarden Shaw
Ipsden
Oxfordshire, England
May 1966

Poems in Periodicals During Owen's Lifetime

'Song of Songs', *The Hydra*, 1 September 1917, p. 13.
'Miners', *The Nation*, 16 January 1918, p. 539.
'Futility', *The Nation*, 15 June 1918, p. 284.
'Hospital Barge at Cérisy', *The Nation*, 15 June 1918, p. 284.

Posthumous Poems in Periodicals

'The End', *The Saturday Westminster Gazette*, 15 November 1919, p. 17.

'Mental Cases', *Coterie No. 3*, December 1919, p. 50.

'Insensibility', *The Athenaeum*, 16 January 1920, p. 71.

'Greater Love', *Arts and Letters*, III (Spring 1920), 6.

'Arms and the Boy', *Arts and Letters*, III (Spring 1920), 9.

'The Next War', *Arts and Letters*, III (Spring 1920), 9.

'Fragment', *The Athenaeum*, 13 August 1920, p. 201. [Variants of 18 lines of 'Strange Meeting'.]

'Asleep', *The London Mercury*, V (November 1921), 12.

Posthumous Poems in Anthologies

'Strange Meeting', 'The Show', 'A Terre', 'The Sentry', 'Disabled', 'The Dead-Beat', 'The Chances', *Wheels, 1919: Fourth Cycle,* edited by Edith Sitwell, Oxford: Blackwell, 1919, pp. 52-64.

Editions of Owen's Books

Poems. With an Introduction by Siegfried Sassoon. London: Chatto & Windus, 1920. xii, 33 pp. Portrait.
Contains:
'Strange Meeting'
'Greater Love'
'Apologia pro Poemate Meo'
'The Show'
'Mental Cases'
'Parable of the Old Men and the Young'
'Arms and the Boy'
'Anthem for Doomed Youth'
'The Send-Off'
'Insensibility'
'Dulce et Decorum Est'
'The Sentry'
'The Dead-Beat'
'Exposure'
'Spring Offensive'
'The Chances'
'S. I. W.'
'Futility'
'Smile, Smile, Smile'
'Conscious'
'A Terre'

'Wild with All Regrets'
'Disabled'
Reprinted 1921 with the addition of 'The End.'
American edition: New York: B. W. Heubsch, 1921. xii, 33 pp. Portrait.

Poems. A New Edition, Including Many Pieces Now First Published, and
Notices of His Life and Work, by Edmund Blunden. London: Chatto &
Windus, 1931, vii, 135 pp. Portrait.
Contains:
'From My Diary, July 1914'
'The Unreturning'
'To Eros'
'My Shy Hand'
'Storm'
'Music'
'Shadwell Stair'
'Happiness'
'Exposure'
'Fragment: Cramped in That Funnelled Hole'
'Fragment: It Is Not Death'
'The Parable of the Old Men and the Young'
'Arms and the Boy'
'The Show'
'The Send-Off'

13

14

'Six O'Clock in Princes Street'
'The Roads Also'
'This Is the Track'
'The Calls'
'Miners'
'And I Must Go'
'The Promisers'
'Training'
'The Kind Ghosts'
'To My Friend'
'Inspection'
'Fragment: A Farewell'
'Fragment: The Abyss of War'
'At a Calvary Near the Ancre'
'Le Christianisme'
'Spring Offensive'
'The Sentry'
'Smile, Smile, Smile'
'The End'
'Strange Meeting'
Reprinted 1933 in the Phoenix Library, with corrections. Without
    portrait.
Reprinted 1939.

Reprinted 1946. Without portrait. Reprinted 1949, 1951, 1955, 1960, 1961, 1963, 1964.

American edition: New York: The Viking Press, 1931. vii, 135 pp. Portrait.

Reprinted 1949 by New Directions, New York and Norwalk, Conn., in The New Classics Series.

Thirteen Poems. With Drawings by Ben Shahn. Northampton, Mass.: Gehenna Press, 1956. 26 pp. 400 copies.

Contains:

'The Parable of the Old Men & the Young'

'Miners'

'Spring Offensive'

'Futility'

'My Shy Hand'

'Strange Meeting'

'Fragment: The Abyss of War'

'Greater Love'

'Apologia Pro Poemate Meo'

'Exposure'

'Six O'Clock in Princes Street'

'Song of Songs'

'Wild with All Regrets'

The Collected Poems. Edited with an Introduction and Notes by C. Day Lewis, and with a Memoir by Edmund Blunden. London: Chatto & Windus, 1963. 191 pp.

Contains:

'Strange Meeting'

'Insensibility'

'Apologia Pro Poemate Meo'

'Greater Love'

'The Parable of the Old Men and the Young'

'Arms and the Boy'

'Anthem for Doomed Youth'

'The Send-Off'

'Exposure'

'The Show'

'Spring Offensive'

'Dulce et Decorum Est'

'Asleep'

'Futility'

'The Last Laugh'

'The Letter'

'The Sentry'

'Conscious'

'A Terre'

'Disabled'

18

'Sonnet Autumnal'
'Long Ages Past'
'Purple'
'Maundy Thursday'
'To ----'
'Spells and Incantation (a Fragment)'
'The Imbecile'
'Beauty'
'Bold Horatius'
'Elegy in April and September'
'To a Comrade in Flanders'
'Wild with All Regrets'
Reprinted 1963.
Reprinted 1964 (twice).
American edition: New York: New Directions, 1964. A New Directions
   Book.

Poems Reprinted in Periodicals

'A Terre', *Literary Digest*, LXVIII (26 March 1921), 36.

'Anthem for Doomed Youth', *Literary Digest*, LXVIII (26 March 1921), 36.

'Anthem for Doomed Youth', *Scholastic*, XLII (1-6 March 1943), 19. (With unsigned commentary.]

'Dulce et Decorum Est', *Scholastic*, XXV (10 November 1934), 11. *[*With unsigned commentary.]

'The End', *The Living Age*, CCCIII (13 December 1919), 682.

'Futility', *Forum*, XCIV (14 December 1935), supplement.

'Futility', *Scholastic*, XXXIII (5 November 1938), 21E.

'Greater Love', *The Living Age*, CCCVIII (12 February 1921), 434.

'Greater Love', *Literary Digest*, LXVIII (26 March 1921), 36.

'Our Brains Ache' *[*'Exposure'*]*, *London Mercury*, XIX (January 1929), 299-300.

'Preferences', *Canadian Forum*, XII (November 1931), 58.

'The Sentry', *Scholastic, XXXIII* (5 November 1938), 21E.

'Strange Meeting', *Literary Digest*, LXVIII (26 March 1921), 36.

Poems Translated into French

'Étranger Rencontre', translated by Henrietta Arnaud, *Anthologie de la Poésie Anglaise Contemporaine*, poèmes choisis et présentés par G.-A. Astre, Paris: L'Arche, 1949, pp. 58-62.

'Disabled', translated by Louis Bonnerot, *Yggdrasill* (Paris), juillet-aout 1939, pp. 256-257.

'Mutilé', translated by Louis Bonnerot and A. Brulé, *Mercure de France*, CCXCIV (15 septembre 1939), 689-690. [With commentary.]

See Gerard Hardin, below.

Poems Translated into Spanish

Poesía Inglesa Contemporánea: Antología. Translated *[*into Spanish*]* by
William Shand and Alberto Girri. Buenos Aires: Nova, 1948. 98 pp.
*[*Includes Wilfred Owen.*]*

Letters

Collected Letters of Wilfred Owen, edited by John Bell and Harold Owen. London: Oxford University Press, to be published.

Applejoy, Petronius. 'Wilfred Owen Denounces War', *Catholic World*, CXLVI (March 1938), 679-684.

B., E. See Reviews, below.

Bateson, F. W. *English Poetry: A Critical Introduction*. London: Longmans, Green, 1950, p. 234.

.... *English Poetry and the English Language*. [Oxford, 1934.] Second Edition. New York: Russell & Russell, 1961, pp. 121-122.

Bayley, John. 'But for Beaumont-Hamel . . .', *Spectator*, CCXI (4 October 1963), 419-420. *[Review-article of The Collected Poems.]*

.... *The Romantic Survival: A Study in Poetic Evolution*. London: Constable, 1957, pp. 86-90. *[A comparison of Yeats and Owen.]*

Benet, William Rose. 'Owen, Wilfred (1893-1918)', *The Reader's Encylopedia*. New York: Thomas Y. Crowell, 1948, p. 809.

.... See Reviews, below.

Bergonzi, Bernard. 'Rosenberg and Owen,' *Heroes' Twilight: A Study of the Literature of the Great War*. London: Constable, 1965, pp. 109-135.

Blackburn, Thomas. *The Price of an Eye*. London: Longmans, Green & Co. Ltd., 1961, pp. 99-100.

Blunden, Edmund. 'Mainly Wilfred Owen', *War Poets, 1914-1918*. London: Longmans, Green & Co., for the British Council and the National Book League (Writers and Their Work, No. 100), 1958, pp. 32-39.

.... 'Memoir of Wilfred Owen', in *Literature for Our Time: An Anthology for College Freshmen*, edited by L. S. Brown, H. O. Waite, and B. P. Atkinson. New York: Henry Holt and Company, 1947, pp. 471-477.

.... See *Poems,* and *The Complete Poems,* above.

Bonnerot, Louis. See Reviews, below.

Braithwaite, William S. See Reviews, below.

Brown, T. J. 'English Literary Autographs XLVIII: Wilfred Owen, 1893-1918', *The Book Collector,* XII (Winter 1963), 489. *[A fair copy of the closing lines of 'Strange Meeting' contains a few important changes. B.M. Add. MSS 43720-1.]*

Bushnell, Athalie. 'Wilfred Owen', *Poetry Review,* XXXVII (No. 3, 1946), 179-184.

Cazamian, Louis. *Symbolisme et poésie: l'exemple anglais.* Paris: La Presse française et étrangère; Oreste Zeluck, éditeur, 1947, pp. 240-243.

Cecil, David, and Allen Tate, editors. *Modern Verse in English, 1900-1950, with Critical Introductions on British and American Poetry and Biographical Notes on the Poets Included.* New York: The Macmillan Company (London: Eyre and Spottiswoode), 1958, pp. 31, 365-370, 637-638. (Includes six Owen poems, a reference to Owen and Sassoon as the 'two most memorable poets of the later war years', and a note that 'Owen. . .experimented a little with assonances and half lines but wrote for the most part in a traditional and romantic manner, derived from Keats. It is the passion and pity that fill his heart that make his poems so deeply memorable'.)

Cejp, Ladislav. 'Nekolik rysu básnického díla Wilfreda Owena' ('Some Characteristics of Wilfred Owen's Poetry'), *Casopis pro moderni filologii,* XXXII (1949), 181-189.

.... 'Podivné setkání: Glossy k básni Wilfreda Owena', *Sborník Vysoké skoly pedagogické v Olomouci*, IV (1957), 185-193.

.... 'Wilfred Owen: Profil válecneho básnika' ('Wilfred Owen: Profile of a Great War Poet') *Slovesná Veda*, II (1949), 24-28.

Church, Richard. See Reviews, below.

Churchill, R. C. 'The Age of T. S. Eliot', in *The Concise Cambridge History of English Literature*, by George Sampson. Cambridge: At the University Press, 1961, pp. 959-960, 971. *[Second edition.]*

Cohen, Joseph. 'In Memory of W. B. Yeats — and Wilfred Owen', *JEGP*, LVIII (October 1959), 637-649; errata, LIX (January 1960), 171.

.... 'Owen Agonistes', *English Literature in Transition* (1880-1920), VIII (December 1965), 253-268. [Reprinted as a pamphlet, 24 pp.]

.... 'Owen's "The Show" ', *The Explicator*, XVI (November 1957), Item No. 8.

.... 'The War Poet as Archetypal Spokesman', *Stand* (Leeds), IV (No. 3, 1964), 23-27. *[The entire issue was devoted to 'The War Poets'.]*

.... 'The Wilfred Owen War Poetry Collection', *Library Chronicle of the University of Texas*, V (Spring 1955), 24-35.

.... 'Wilfred Owen: Fresher Fields than Flanders', *English Literature in Transition (1880-1920)*, VII (No. 1, 1964), 1-7.

.... 'Wilfred Owen in America', *Prairie Schooner*, XXXI (Winter 1957), 339-345.

.... 'Wilfred Owen's Greater Love', *Tulane Studies in English*, VI (1956), 105-117.

27

.... 'Wilfred Owen's Manuscripts', *Times Literary Supplement*, 10 August 1956, p. 475. [See D. S. R. Welland, below].

.... 'Wilfred Owen's Tombstone Inscription Reconsidered'. Pamphlet, 1956 (?), 4 pp.

Coleman, John. See Reviews, below.

Collins, H. P. *Modern Poetry*. London: Jonathan Cape; Boston: Houghton Mifflin and Company, 1925.

Cooke, Deryck. 'Bad Rhymes', *New Statesman*, 4 September 1964, p. 318. *[Says Owen did not rhyme badly.]*

Daiches, David. *A Critical History of English Literature*. New York: The Ronald Press Company, 1960, pp. 1115-1116.

.... *Poetry and the Modern World: A Study of Poetry in England Between 1900 and 1939*. Chicago: The University of Chicago Press, 1940, pp. 65-71, 192, 201, 214.

.... 'The Poetry of Wilfred Owen', *New Literary Values: Studies in Modern Literature*. Edinburgh *[etc.]*: Oliver and Boyd, 1936, pp. 52-68.

Davie, Donald. 'In the Pity', *New Statesman*, 28 August 1964, pp. 282-283.

Deutsch, Babette. *Poetry in Our Time*. New York: Columbia University Press, 1956, pp. 348-352, *et passim;* Garden City, New York: Doubleday & Company, Inc., 1963, pp. 390-392 *et passim*.

.... See Reviews, below.

Dickinson, Patric. 'Poetry of Wilfred Owen', *Fortnightly*, CLXII (n.s. CLVI) (November 1944), 327-331.

28

.... *The Good Minute: An Autobiographical Study*. London: Victor Gollancz Ltd., 1965, pp. 118-126, *et passim*.

D*[*obrée*]*, B*[*onamy*]*. 'Owen, Wilfred', in *The Concise Encyclopedia of English and American Poets and Poetry*, edited by Stephen Spender and Donald Hall. New York: Hawthorn Books, Inc., 1963, pp. 235-236; photograph, p. 338. *[*Refers to Owen as 'the outstanding poet of the First World War'.*]*

Durrell, Lawrence. *A Key to Modern British Poetry*. London: Peter Nevill Ltd., 1952, pp. 133-135.

Eagle, Solomon. 'A New War Poet', *The Living Age*, CCCVIII (5 February 1921), 370-371. *[*From *The Outlook;* 'Eagle' is Sir John C. Squire.*]*

Emerson, Dorothy. 'Poetry Corner', *Scholastic*, XXV (10 November 1934), 11.

.... 'Poetry Corner', *Scholastic*, XXXIII (5 November 1938), 21E.

Enright, D. J. 'The Literature of the First World War', in *The Modern Age*, edited by Boris Ford. Vol. *7* of *Pelican Guide to English Literature*. Baltimore: Pelican Books, 1961, pp. 154-169; London: Cassell, 1964, pp. 154-169.

.... 'My Subject Is War', *Spectator*, CCV (18 November 1960), 785-786. *[*Review-article of D. S. R. Welland's *Wilfred Owen.]*

.... See Reviews, below.

Evans, B. Ifor. 'War and the Writer', *English Literature Between the Wars*. London: Methuen & Co. Ltd., 1949, pp. 102-113 (see pp. 103-105). *[*Second edition.*]*

Fairchild, Hoxie Neale. 'Toward Hysteria', *Religious Trends in English*

Poetry, Vol. V, 1880-1920. New York: Columbia University Press, 1962, pp. 578-627.

Fletcher, Ifan Kyrle. 'Wilfred Owen', *Welsh Outlook*, XV (November 1928), 332-333.

Fletcher, James G. See Reviews, below.

Fletcher, John. 'Wilfred Owen Re-edited', *Études Anglaises*, XVII (avril-juin 1964), 171-178.

Fowler, Albert. 'The Pity Is the Music: Benjamin Britten's *War Requiem*', *Approach*, No. 50 (Winter 1965), pp. 40-44. *[Britten's setting of Wilfred Owen's poems is eminently successful.]*

Fraser, G. S. See Reviews below.

Freeman, Rosemary. 'Parody as a Literary Form: George Herbert and Wilfred Owen', *Essays in Criticism*, XIII (October 1963), 307-322. *[On 'Greater Love'.]*

Gardner, Brian, editor. *Up the Line to Death: The War Poets 1914-1918: An Anthology*, with an Introduction and Notes. Foreword by Edmund Blunden. London: Methuen & Co. Ltd., 1964. [Introductory poem and five selections by Wilfred Owen, pp. *[v]*, 136-141; a long note on Owen, pp. 175-176.]

Gose, Elliott B., Jr. 'Digging In: An Interpretation of Wilfred Owen's "Strange Meeting" ', *College English*, XXII (March 1961), 417-419.

Gordon, George. *Poetry and the Moderns*. Oxford: The Clarendon Press, 1935, p. 24.

Graves, Robert. *Good-bye to All That: An Autobiography*. London: Jonathan

Cape, 1929; New York: Jonathan Cape & Harrison Smith, 1930, p. 314; New Edition, London: Cassell & Company Ltd., 1957, p. 234.

Gregory, Horace. See Reviews, below.

Grigson, Geoffrey. See Reviews, below.

Grubb, Frederick. 'The Embattled Truth: Wilfred Owen and Isaac Rosenberg', *A Vision of Reality: A Study in Liberalism in Twentieth-Century Verse*. London: Chatto and Windus, 1965, pp. 73-96.

Hardin, Gérard. 'La passion de Wilfred Owen', *Esprit*, XXIX (septembre 1961), 177- 189. *[Followed by a translation of 'Arms and the Boy', 'Anthem for Doomed Youth', and 'Strange Meeting', pp. 190-192.]*

Hazo, Samuel J. 'The Passion of Wilfred Owen', *Renascence*, XI (Summer 1959), 201-208.

Hill, James J., Jr. 'The Text of Wilfred Owen's "Purple"', *Notes and Queries*, n.s. X (December 1963), 464. *[Last word of line 10 is 'King'.]*

--------------, 'Wilfred Owen's "Greater Love"', *Essays in Criticism*, XV (1965), 476-477. [See Rosemary Freeman, above.]

Hughes, Ted. See Reviews, below.

Johnson, Manly. See Reviews, below.

Johnston, John H. 'Poetry and Pity: Wilfred Owen', *English Poetry of the First World War: A Study in the Evolution of Lyric and Narrative Form*. Princeton: Princeton University Press, 1964, pp. 155-209.

Kunitz, Stanley J., 'Poet of the War', *Poetry* XL (June 1932), 159-162. *[Review-article of Poems, 1931.]*

................, editor. 'Wilfred Owen, 1893-1918', *Authors Today and Yesterday.* New York: The H. W. Wilson Company, 1933, pp. 509-511.

................, and Howard Haycraft. 'Owen, Wilfred', *Twentieth Century Authors.* New York: The H. W. Wilson Company, 1942, pp. 1061-1062.

Landon, George McQueen. 'The Contribution of Grammar to the Poetic Style of Wilfred Owen', *Dissertation Abstracts,* XXV (1965), 6610. [Indiana University Ph. D. thesis.]

Lahey, G. F. 'Wilfred Owen', *Canadian Bookman,* XV (October 1933), 133-134.

Larkin, Philip. See Reviews, below.

Ledward, Patricia. 'The Poetry of Wilfred Owen', *Poetry Review,* XXXII (March-April, 1941), 99-108.

Levi, Peter. See Reviews, below.

Lewis, C. Day. *A Hope for Poetry.* London: Oxford University Press, 1934, pp. 2-3, 15, *et passim.*

.... See *The Complete Poems,* above.

Lewis, Naomi. See Reviews, below.

Loiseau, J. 'A Reading of Wilfred Owen's Poems', *English Studies,* XXI (June 1939), 97-108.

McDonald, Gerald. See Reviews, below.

MacNeice, Louis. See Reviews, below.

Masson, David I. 'Wilfred Owen's Free Phonetic Patterns: Their Style and Function', *Journal of Aesthetics and Art Criticism,* XIII (March 1955), 360-369.

Matthews, Geoffrey. 'Brooke and Owen', *Stand,* IV (No. 3, 1964), 28-34.

Maxwell, J. C. See Reviews, below.

Milne, H. J. M. 'The Poems of Wilfred Owen', *British Museum Quarterly*, IX (1935), 19-20.

Morrison, Theodore. See Reviews, below.

Muir, Edwin. *['Wilfred Owen'.] The Present Age from 1914*. London: The Cressett Press, 1939, pp. 85, 86, 93-95, 189, 210, 301.

Murry, J. Middleton. See Reviews, below.

----------------, 'The Present Condition of Poetry', *Aspects of Literature*. New York: Alfred A. Knopf, 1920, pp. 139-149. [Reprinted from *Athenaeum*, December 1919; comments on 'Strange Meeting' in *Wheels*; see pp. 145-147.]

Nichols, Robert. See Reviews, below.

Norman, Charles. 'To the Memory of Wilfred Owen', *Bookman* (New York), LXVIII (November 1928), 316-317. *[Poem.]*

Olson, Lawrence. See Reviews, below.

Owen, Harold. *Journey from Obscurity: Wilfred Owen 1893-1918, Memoirs of the Owen Family: I. Childhood*. London: Oxford University Press, 1963. xiii, 274 pp.; *II. Youth*. London: Oxford University Press, 1964. ix, 292 pp.; *III. War*. London: Oxford University Press, 1965. xi, 263 pp.

Parsons, I. M. 'The Poems of Wilfred Owen (1893-1918)', *New Criterion*, X (July 1931), 658-669.

----------------, editor. *Men Who March Away: Poems of the First World War*. London: Chatto & Windus, 1965. *[Not only does Owen have more poems (13) in this anthology than any of the 33 writers, but he is prominently mentioned in the Introduction, pp. 13-28.]*

Pinto, V. de Sola. *Crisis in English Poetry, 1880-1940*. London: Hutchinson's University Library, 1951.

Porter, Alan. See Reviews, below.

Roberts, Michael, editor. *Faber Book of Modern Verse*. London: Faber & Faber, 1936, p. 28.

Ross, Robert H. *The Georgian Revolt 1910-1922: Rise and Fall of a Poetic Ideal*. Carbondale: Southern Illinois University Press, 1965, pp. 75, 146, 151, 175, 187.

Routh, H. V. 'Sassoon, Owen, Blunden', *English Literature and Ideas in the Twentieth Century*. London: Methuen & Co. Ltd., 1948, pp. 127-128. *[Second edition.]*

S., C. See Reviews, below.

Sassoon, Siegfried. *Siegfried's Journey 1916-1920*. New York: The Viking Press, 1946, pp. 86-102, 106-109. *[Contains excerpts of letters from Owen.]*
.... See *Poems*, above.

Savage, D. S. 'Two Prophetic Poems', *Western Review*, XIII (Winter 1949), 67-78. *[On Yeats and Owen.]*

Sergeant, Howard. 'The Importance of Wilfred Owen', *English*, X (Spring 1954), 9-12.

Seymour-Smith, Martin. See Reviews, below.

Silkin, Jon. 'Owen, Rosenberg & the War', *Stand*, VI (No. 4, 1966?), 26-42. [Review-article of *The Collected Poems* and D.S.R. Welland's *Wilfred Owen*.]

34

Sitwell, Edith. *Trio: Dissertations on Some Aspects of National Genius.* London: Macmillan, 1938, p. 143.

Sitwell, Osbert. 'Wilfred Owen', *Atlantic*, CLXXXVI (August 1950), 37-42. *[Excerpt from Noble Essences. Reprinted in Jubilee: One Hundred Years of the 'Atlantic', selected and edited by Edward Weeks and Emily Flint. Boston, Toronto: Little, Brown and Company, 1957, pp. 468-477.]*

Slavit, David R. See Reviews, below.

Spear, Hilda D. 'Wilfred Owen and Poetic Truth', *University of Kansas City Review*, XXV (Winter 1958), 110-116.

Spender, Stephen. 'Poetry and Pity', *The Destructive Element*. Boston: Houghton Mifflin and Company, 1936, pp. 217-221.

S[quire], J. C. See Reviews, below.

Strachan, R. H. *The Soul of Modern Poetry*. London: Hodder and Stoughton Limited, 1922, pp. 160-163.

Swinnerton, Frank. 'War-time Afflatus', *The Georgian Scene: A Literary Panorama*. New York: Farrar & Rinehart, 1934, pp. 317-336. *[See pp. 325-327; English edition, pp. 262-264.]*

Thomas, Dylan. 'Wilfred Owen', *Quite Early One Morning*. London: J. M. Dent & Sons Ltd., 1954, pp. 91-105; New York: New Directions, 1954, pp. 117-133.

--------------- 'The Welshman as Poet', *Atlantic*, CXCIV (November 1954), 76-84; see p. 80.

Thomas, R. George. See Reviews, below.

Thompson, Marjorie, and John Gross. See Reviews, below.

Thwaite, Anthony. *Contemporary English Poetry: An Introduction*. London: Heinemann, 1959.

Tindall, William York. *Forces in Modern British Literature 1885-1946*. New York: Alfred A. Knopf, 1947, p. 120.

Tomlinson, Charles. See Reviews, below.

Untermeyer, Louis. 'Wilfred Owen', *Lives of the Poets: The Story of One Thousand Years of English and American Poetry*. New York: Simon and Schuster, 1959, pp. 692-695. *['Of the English poets Sassoon, Graves, Blunden, Brooke, Rosenberg, and Sorley, it was Wilfred Owen who made the greatest impression on the next generation as well as his own'.]*

.... See Reviews, below (2).

Vallette, Jacques. 'Trois poètes anglaises morts à la guerre', *Mercure de France*, No. 1004 (1er avril 1947), pp. 641-654. *[On Owen, Lewis, and Keyes.]*

Van Doren, Carl, and Mark Van Doren. 'Owen 1893-1918', *American and British Literature Since 1890*. New York and London: D. Appleton-Century Company, 1939, pp. 186-187.

Van Doren, Mark. See Reviews, below.

Wain, John. See Reviews, below.

Walsh, T. J., Editor. *A Tribute to Wilfred Owen*. [Birkenhead: Birkenhead Institute, 1964.] 62 pp.

Welland, D. S. R. 'Half-Rhyme in Wilfred Owen: Its Derivation and Use', *Review of English Studies*, n.s. I (July 1950), 226-241.

.... 'Wilfred Owen', *Times Literary Supplement,* 19 July 1947, p. 369. *[*See Harold Owen, *TLS,* 18 October 1947, p. 535.*]*

.... *Wilfred Owen: A Critical Study.* London: Chatto & Windus, 1960. 159 pp.

.... 'Wilfred Owen: Poetry, Pity and Prophecy', *Northern Review* (Montreal), VI (October-November 1953), 29-36.

.... 'Wilfred Owen's Manuscripts', *Times Literary Supplement,* 15 June 1956, p. 368; 22 June, p. 384. *[*See also letters by Edith Sitwell, *TLS,* 22 June, p. 377; Joseph Cohen, 10 August, p. 475; author's reply, 17 August, p. 487.*]*

White, Gertrude M. *Wilfred Owen.* Twayne English Authors Series. New York: Twayne Publishers, to be published.

Wulfsberg, Fredrik. 'Han som kastet medaljen pa sjoen', *Samtiden,* LXXII (May 1963), 238-252. *[*In Norwegian. Before Siegfried Sassoon returned to the front he had a conversation with Wilfred Owen.*]*

Yeats, William Butler. *Letters on Poetry to Dorothy Wellesley.* New York: Oxford University Press, 1940, p. 124.

Unsigned. 'Lost Identities', *Times Literary Supplement,* 27 February 1959, p. 113. *[*Letters and juvenilia of Owen made available to Patric Dickinson 'an invaluable group of new material'.*]*

.... 'Wilfred Owen Against the Background of Two Wars', *Times Literary Supplement,* 28 August 1953, p. xxvii. *[*'Thoughts and Second Thoughts,' Special Autumn Number.*]*

Reviews of Books by and about Owen

Poems, 1920, 1921.

B., E. *Athenaeum,* 10 December 1920, p. 807.

Benet, William Rose. *Yale Review,* n.s. XI (October 1921), 179.

Braithwaite, William S. *Boston Transcript,* 5 May 1921, p. 6.

Fletcher, James G. *Freeman,* III (1 June 1921), 282.

Murry, J. Middleton. *The Nation and Athenaeum,* XXVIII (19 February 1921), 705-707.

Nichols, Robert. *Springfield Republican,* 30 January 1921, p. 5a. *[From London Observer.]*

S[quire], J. C. *London Mercury,* III (January 1921), 334-335.

Untermeyer, Louis. *Literary Review, New York Evening Post,* 30 April 1921, p. 4.

Van Doren, Mark. *The Nation* (New York), CXII (25 May 1921), 747.

Unsigned. *A.L.A. Booklist,* XVII (May 1921), 294.

.... *Daily Chronicle* (London), 8 December 1920, p. 6.

.... *The Dial,* LXXI (July 1921), 120.

.... *New York Times Book Review,* 15 May 1921, p. 13.

.... *Spectator,* CXXV (18 December 1920), 821.

.... *Times Literary Supplement,* 16 December 1920, p. 862.

.... *Times Literary Supplement,* 6 January 1921, p. 6.

Poems, 1931.

Bonnerot, Louis. *La revue anglo-américaine,* IX (juin 1932), 452-453.

Church, Richard. *New Statesman and Nation,* I (11 April 1931), 256.

Gregory, Horace, *The Nation* (New York), CXXXIII (25 November 1931), 577-578.

Grigson, Geoffrey. *Saturday Review* (London), CLII (18 July 1931), 95.

Kunitz, Stanley J. *Poetry*, XL (June 1932), 159-162.
Morrison, Theodore. *Atlantic*, CXLIX (June 1932), 14.
Porter, Alan. *Voices*, V (January 1931), 93.
Untermeyer, Louis. *Saturday Review of Literature*, VIII (12 September 1931), 114.
Unsigned. *A.L.A. Booklist*, XXVIII (November 1931), 119.
.... *Boston Transcript*, 14 October 1931, p. 3.
.... *Spectator*, CXLVI (6 June 1931), 905.
.... *Times Literary Supplement*, 4 June 1931, p. 443.

Poems, 1949.

Deutsch, Babette. *New York Herald Tribune Book Review*, 1 January 1950, p. 6.
Johnson, Manly. *Hopkins Review*, III (No. 2, 1950), 55.
McDonald, Gerald. *Library Journal*, LXXIV (15 December 1949), 1909.
Olson, Lawrence. *Furioso*, V (No. 4, 1950), 75.
Unsigned. *Virginia Kirkus Bookshop Service*, XVII (15 November 1949), 644.

The Collected Poems, 1963.

Bayley, John. *Spectator*, CCXI (4 October 1963), 419-420.
Enright, D. J. *New Statesman*, LXVI (27 September 1963), 408-410.
Fraser, G. S. *New York Review of Books*, 19 March 1964, pp. 6-7.
Hughes, Ted. *New York Times Books*, 12 April 1964, pp. 4, 18.
Larkin, Philip. *The Listener*, LXX (10 October 1963), 561-562.
Levi, Peter. *Tablet*, 26 October 1963, p. 1146.
Silkin, Jon. *Stand*, VI (No. 4, 1966?), 26-42.

Slavit, David R. *New York Herald Tribune Books,* 13 September 1964, pp. 18-19.

Tomlinson, Charles. *Poetry,* CIV (April 1964), 41-43.

Unsigned. *Time,* LXXXIII (29 May 1964), 90-92.

.... *Times Literary Supplement,* 7 November 1963, p. 908.

Wilfred Owen: A Critical Study, by D. S. R. Welland.

Coleman, John. *The Sunday Times* (London), 2 October 1960, p. 27.

MacNeice, Louis. *New Statesman,* LX (1960), 623-624.

Maxwell, J. C. *Notes & Queries,* o.s. CCVII, (n.s. IX) (March 1962), 119.

Silkin, Jon. *Stand,* VI (No. 4, 1966?), 26-42.

Thomas, R. George. *Review of English Studies,* n.s. XIII (February 1962), 89-91.

Thompson, Marjorie, and John Gross. *Year's Work in English Studies,* 1960, pp. 252-253.

Unsigned. *Times Literary Supplement,* 18 November 1960, p. 742.

Journey from Obscurity, by Harold Owen.

Enright, D. J. *New Statesman,* LXVIII (9 October 1964), 542-543.

Lewis, Naomi. *The Listener,* LXXII (5 November 1964), 730.

S., C. *The Glasgow Herald,* 13 November 1965, p. 11.

Seymour-Smith, Martin. Spectator, CCXIII (9 October 1964), 480.

Spear, Hilda D. *English Literature in Transition (1880-1920),* IX (No. 2, 1966), 112-113.

Tomlinson, Charles. *Poetry,* CIV (April 1964), 41-43.

Wain, John. *The Observer Weekend Review,* 10 October 1965.

Unsigned. *The Economist,* CCVIII (6 July 1963), 45.

.... *Times Literary Supplement*, 16 August 1963, p. 626.
[Further reviews of this important work appeared in the *Birmingham* (England) Post, the *Daily Telegraph* (London) (Anthony Powell, *The Guardian* (Manchester), *The Observer* (Harold Nicolson), *Punch* (Joanna Richardson), the *Sunday Telegraph* (William Plomer), *The Sunday Times* (Vol. I, Stephen Spender; Vol. II, Julian Jebb), *Times Educational Supplement*, among others.]

A Tribute to Wilfred Owen, edited by T. J. Walsh.

Unsigned. *Times Literary Supplement*, 17 September 1964, p. 865.

Addendum

Colophon. 'The Wheel of Life', *John O'London's Weekly*, XXXI (30 June 1934), 475. [A weekly columnist who writes, 'There is no doubt about it, if we must talk of "war poets," Wilfred Owen has the first claim to immortality.']

DATE DUE

MAR 7 1974		
1 89		
GAYLORD		PRINTED IN U.S.A.